THE BİG

60

Your Survival Guide

An exclusive edition for

for all your gift books and gift stationery

This edition first published in Great Britain in 2018 by
Allsorted Ltd, Watford, Herts, UK WD19 4BG

© Susanna Geoghegan Gift Publishing

Author: Emma Hill

Cover design: Milestone Creative

ISBN: 978-1-911517-51-1

Printed in China

THE BIG

60

SUPERB
* and *
60

THE BIG 60 IS UPON YOU!

What to do with the next decade of your life?
Firstly, you could dip into this book filled with
witticisms, truths, jokes and advice on turning 60.
Sure, we can look back on your 40s and 50s with
wistful nostalgia; those heady days when you
managed to visit friends' houses without taking
your slippers, but mostly we're looking ahead with
optimism and enthusiasm, comfortable in our own
skin, definitely wiser and ready to embark on a
later-life adventure. Don't let getting older drag
you down (who knows how long it will take you to
get back up again), embrace your sensational
sixties and let life begin!

YOU KNOW YOU ARE 60 WHEN...

- You make an 'oof' noise when getting up

- You have no idea who all these youngster celebrities are...and you couldn't care less

- You discuss cleaning products with your friends

- You wake up early when you could have had a lie-in

- You remember all the songs from the first time around

- You start doing retirement maths on your commute to work

- You refer to 'taping' your favourite television programmes

- A garden centre is your idea of a good day out

- You can't remember what you said to someone yesterday, but you can remember the jingle from a 1960s advert

YOU SEND MORE LETTERS OF COMPLAINT THAN EMAILS

YOUR FACE IS MARKED WITH LINES OF LIFE, PUT THERE BY LOVE AND LAUGHTER, SUFFERING AND TEARS. IT'S BEAUTIFUL.

LYNSAY SANDS

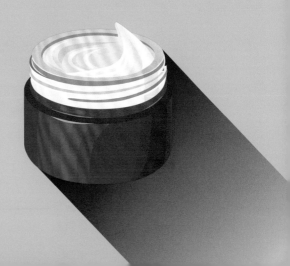

A WORD FROM THE WISE

One starts to get young at the age of sixty and then it is too late.
Pablo Picasso

I believe the second half of one's life is meant to be better than the first half. The first half is finding out how you do it. And the second half is enjoying it.
Frances Lear

At any age it does us no harm to look over our past shortcomings and plan to improve our characters and actions in the coming year.
Eleanor Roosevelt

Age is a matter of feeling...not of years.
George William Curtis

You are not too old and it is not too late.
Unknown

60s & 70s TRIVIA
(PART 1)

1. The Beatles gave their first live American television performance on which show?

2. Which model was voted the face of 1966?

3. Who bought the News of the World in 1969?

4. 'Jumpin' Jack Flash' was a hit for The Rolling Stones in which year?

5. In 1967, who was captured and executed by the Bolivian army?

6. Who sang the theme song to the film Born Free?

7. Which famous sporting and entertainment venue opened in New York in February 1968?

8. What was the name of Stephen King's first published novel, released in 1974?

9. Which president resigned in 1974 over the Watergate scandal?

10. Which music festival was held at Max Yasgur's 600-acre dairy farm in 1969?

(See page 94 for answers)

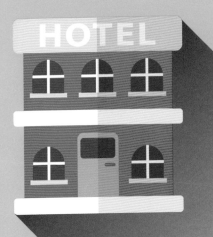

THINGS TO DO NOW YOU'RE 60

- Plant a garden

- Take up pilates

- Learn a new language with your partner and speak it in the house

- Buy an exquisite piece of jewellery

- Re-connect with an old friend

- Travel the world

- Volunteer in your community

- Create your own recipe book

- Get a pet

LEARN TO PAINT

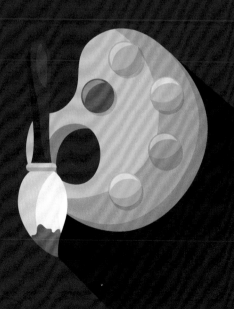

FOR ALL THE ADVANCES IN MEDICINE, THERE IS STILL NO CURE FOR THE COMMON BIRTHDAY.

JOHN GLENN

YOU'RE HAVING A LAUGH

Retirement must be wonderful. I mean, you can suck in your stomach for only so long.
Burt Reynolds

Patient: Doctor! I have a serious problem; I can never remember what I just said.
Doctor: When did you first notice this problem?
Patient: What problem?

You know you are getting old when you stoop down to tie your shoes and wonder what else you can do while you're down there.
George Burns

The secret of staying young is to live honestly, eat slowly, and lie about your age.
Lucille Ball

Time flies like an arrow. Fruit flies like a banana.
Groucho Marx

WE DON'T GROW OLDER, WE GROW RIPER.

PABLO PICASSO

A WORD FROM THE WISE

To be happy, we must be true to nature, and carry our age along with us.
William Hazlitt

He who is of a calm and happy nature will hardly feel the pressure of age, but to him who is of an opposite disposition, youth and age are equally a burden.
Plato

Know that you are the perfect age. Each year is special and precious for you shall only live it once.
Louise Hay

Age does not depend upon years, but upon temperament and health. Some men are born old, and some never grow up.
Tryon Edwards

Age is how we determine how valuable you are.
Jane Elliot

DID YOU KNOW?

Several studies have shown that working past retirement age can help you achieve longevity, so perhaps don't give up the day job just yet...

Squinting to read your paper? More powerful reading glasses aren't necessarily the answer - try turning on the lights! In general, 60-year-olds need three times as much light to comfortably read in as 20-year-olds

By now you've probably developed 'crystallized intelligence' - i.e. you've got good at using what you've learnt over the years.

BY 60 YEARS OF AGE, AROUND 60 PER CENT OF MEN AND 40 PER CENT OF WOMEN WILL BEGIN TO SNORE WHEN SLEEPING. SNORES AVERAGE AROUND 60 DECIBELS, THE NOISE LEVEL OF NORMAL SPEECH, BUT CAN REACH MORE THAN 80 DECIBELS.

PASS THE EARPLUGS, DEAR.

60 THINGS YOU SHOULD KNOW BY THE TIME YOU TURN 60 (PART 1)

- Your health is your real wealth

- It's never too late

- Kindness is more important than anything

- You are in charge of your own happiness

- To be gentle with yourself

- How to get rid of things that are neither useful nor beautiful

- How to mind your own business

- Keep it simple

- To check your teeth after eating seedy bread

HOW TO CHANGE A TYRE

YOU'RE NEVER TOO OLD

Peter Roget didn't even start working on his thesaurus until he was 61.

Playwright and essayist George Bernard Shaw finished writing Heartbreak House, regarded by many as his masterpiece, at the age of 60.

At the age of 63, Elizabeth Kingsley created the double-crostic puzzle (now known as an acrostic puzzle).

At 68, French President Charles de Gaulle, who had resigned 12 years earlier, made a political comeback.

AT THE AGE OF 60, ITALIAN SCULPTOR, PAINTER, PLAYWRIGHT, DRAFTSMAN AND ARCHITECT GIAN LORENZO BERNINI BEGAN DESIGNING CHURCHES.

YOU KNOW YOU ARE 60 WHEN...

- You get into heated arguments over pension plans
- You take your slippers with you when you visit friends' houses
- You talk about your joints
- Sometimes, you just need to sit down
- You take a keen interest in the weather forecast
- You're considering a cruise holiday
- Your knees crack
- Comfort has overtaken style
- You're convinced the doctor, police-officer, etc, look too young to be fully qualified

YOU TAKE A FLASK OF TEA ON A DAY OUT

I THINK THAT, FOR ALL OF US, AS WE GROW OLDER, WE MUST DISCIPLINE OURSELVES TO CONTINUE EXPANDING, BROADENING, LEARNING, KEEPING OUR MINDS ACTIVE AND OPEN.

CLINT EASTWOOD

A WORD FROM THE WISE

The maturity of sixty would be better spent if it came at age twenty.
Dane Peddigrew

I'm not interested in age. People who tell me their age are silly. You're as old as you feel.
Henri-Frédéric Amiel

Don't let age control your life. Let your life control your age.
Anthony Douglas Williams

Those who improve with age embrace the power of personal growth and personal achievement and begin to replace youth with wisdom, innocence with understanding, and lack of purpose with self-actualization.
Bo Bennett

60s & 70s TRIVIA
(PART 2)

1. Name the pair arrested in 1965 on suspicion of running a protection racket in London.

2. Sonny & Cher had a UK number one hit in which year with 'I Got You Babe'?

3. In July 1969, Charles, Prince of Wales, was invested with his title at which Welsh castle?

4. 'Raindrops Keep Fallin' on My Head' was a song written for which 1969 film?

5. Which former first lady married Greek shipping tycoon Aristotle Onassis in 1968?

6. The Beatles released the last album they recorded together in 1969. What was it called?

7. During which Apollo spaceflight did an oxygen tank explode?

8. Which product became the first to be scanned using a barcode in 1974?

9. What kind of bird took Fleetwood Mac to the top of the UK charts in 1969?

10. Which newspaper heiress took part in a San Francisco bank robbery in April 1974?

(See page 95 for answers)

THINGS TO DO NOW YOU'RE 60

- Try a new sport
- Clear out your clutter
- Indulge in some fine dining
- Do something crazy
- Renew your wedding vows
- Stay in touch with social media
- Develop new relationships
- Have a massage on a regular basis
- Go back to college

GROW YOUR OWN FOOD

AT 60, YOUR FAVOURITE CLASSIC ROCK IS ELEVATOR MUSIC.

YOU'RE HAVING A LAUGH

You have to stay in shape. My grandmother started walking five miles a day when she was 60. She's 97 today and we don't know where the hell she is.
Ellen DeGeneres

The years between fifty and seventy are the hardest. You are always being asked to do things, and yet you are not decrepit enough to turn them down.
T. S. Eliot

Wife: These aren't wrinkles, they're laughter lines.
Husband: Well something must have been bloody hilarious.

Getting older is no problem. You just have to live long enough.
Groucho Marx

I'm pushing 60. That's enough exercise for me.
Mark Twain

60 THINGS YOU SHOULD KNOW BY THE TIME YOU TURN 60 (PART 2)

- To work hard at your relationships
- How not to take yourself too seriously
- To spend time with people who make you feel good
- How to agree to disagree
- How to make peace with your past
- Not to save things for a special occasion – today is special
- However good or bad a situation is, it will change
- The acquisition of material goods brings only temporary pleasure
- Breathing deeply calms the mind

HOW TO TAKE CARE OF YOUR BODY

AGEING IS NOT LOST YOUTH BUT A NEW STAGE OF OPPORTUNITY AND STRENGTH.

BETTY FREIDAN

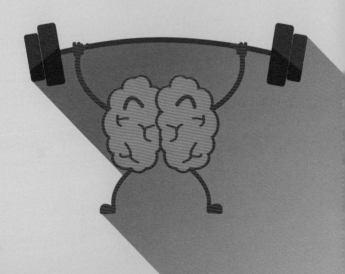

A WORD FROM THE WISE

Age is no guarantee of maturity.
Lawana Blackwell

Age should not have its face lifted, but it should rather teach the world to admire wrinkles as the etchings of experience and the firm line of character.
Clarence Day Jr.

For age is opportunity no less
Than youth itself, though in another dress.
Henry Wadsworth Longfellow

Better pass boldly into that other world, in the full glory of some passion, than fade and wither dismally with age.
James Joyce

The worst old age is that of the mind.
William Hazlitt

DANIEL DEFOE WROTE ROBINSON CRUSOE, HIS FIRST NOVEL AND ARGUABLY THE FIRST-EVER MODERN NOVEL, AT THE AGE OF 60.

YOU'RE NEVER TOO OLD

American journalist and women's rights activist Gloria Steinem, who once famously quipped, 'A woman without a man is like a fish without a bicycle', married for the first time aged 66.

Colonel Sanders started KFC aged 65.

At 63, Jonathan Swift wrote A Modest Proposal, arguably the best satire ever written in English.

60 THINGS YOU SHOULD KNOW BY THE TIME YOU TURN 60 (PART 3)

- It's important to prioritise spending time with positive people

- Not to be judgemental

- How to make small talk in any situation

- Toxic relationships aren't worth it

- How to find and follow your passions

- How to nurture meaningful relationships

- How to give compliments...

- ...and how to accept them

- Don't buy stuff you don't need

SUNSCREEN IS YOUR FRIEND

A WORD FROM THE WISE

Nobody grows old by merely living a number of years. People grow old only by deserting their ideals. Years may wrinkle the skin, but to give up interest wrinkles the soul.
Douglas MacArthur

If you don't learn to laugh at troubles, you won't have anything to laugh at when you grow old.
Ed Howe

Sometimes age succeeds, sometimes it fails. It depends on you.
Ravensara Noite

Count your age by friends, not years. Count your life by smiles, not tears.
John Lennon

Old age and the passage of time teach all things.
Sophocles

DON'T START YOUR DAY WITH THE BROKEN PIECES OF YESTERDAY. EVERY MORNING WE WAKE UP IS THE FIRST DAY OF THE REST OF OUR LIFE.

UNKNOWN

THINGS TO DO NOW YOU'RE 60

- Try a new food
- Take grandchildren on a trip
- Shift to a healthier lifestyle
- Take a leap of faith
- Bury the hatchet
- Do a bungee jump
- Practice yoga
- Make something with your hands...
- ...and sell it on Etsy

ONE GOOD THING ABOUT BEING 60 IS YOU ARGUE LESS. IT'S NOT SO MUCH THAT YOU'RE NICER, YOU JUST CAN'T HEAR EACH OTHER.

UNKNOWN

YOU'RE HAVING A LAUGH

Forget the block, when you're sixty, you've been around the entire neighbourhood a few times.
Dane Peddigrew

Feel the cold now you're getting older? Come sit in the corner…it's 90 degrees!

I recently turned 60. Practically a third of my life is over.
Woody Allen

The tragedy of getting old: So many candles… so little cake.

Getting older has some benefits… Call it a 'senior moment' and you can get away with pretty much anything!

THE AVERAGE 65-YEAR-OLD SEDENTARY WOMAN'S BODY IS 43% FAT COMPARED TO 25% AT AGE 25. CONVERT FAT INTO MUSCLE BY EXERCISING.

DID YOU KNOW?

Your marriage may well be getting better! Married couples in their 60s and beyond score higher in the happiness stakes. Couples often become closer as the years go by, perhaps strengthened by having survived, and therefore bonded over, past stressful life events, or it could be down to an increased ability to communicate and express affection. Either way, it's good news for the old lovebirds among us!

According to the World Health Organization (WHO), the world's population is ageing rapidly, and it expects the number of people aged 60 or older to rise from 900 million worldwide to 2 billion by 2050.

Sleeping patterns shift as we get older. Once you hit your 60s you're likely to wake up with the lark…and be feeling pretty good about it too as most over 60s report getting a good night's sleep on a regular basis. Rise and shine!

60 THINGS YOU SHOULD KNOW BY THE TIME YOU TURN 60 (PART 4)

- Sunglasses are a summer essential, not a fashion statement

- To value your family

- To say thank you...a lot

- How to live within your means

- How to be a good friend

- Happiness is contagious

- It's OK to cry

- Nothing can be gained from worrying

- Don't be wasteful

A CUP OF TEA SOOTHES THE SOUL

DIANA NYAD SWAM FROM CUBA TO FLORIDA – A 110-MILE JOURNEY – AT THE AGE OF 64.

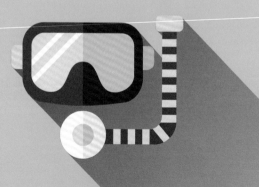

YOU'RE NEVER TOO OLD

At 61, Charles Cagniard de la Tour, a French engineer and physicist, demonstrated that fermentation depends upon yeast cells.

Laura Ingalls Wilder's **Little House on the Prairie** series has long captured the imaginations of schoolchildren, but the books were written when their author was in her golden years - she was 65 years old when the first book was published.

At 67, Simeon Poisson discovered the laws of probability after studying the likelihood of death from mule kicks in the French army.

YOU KNOW YOU ARE 60 WHEN...

- A year feels like 3 months

- The young people in your life look to you for advice

- One's health - or lack of it - crops up more and more in conversations with friends

- You walk into rooms and have no idea what you went in for

- You start getting ID'd again...for OAP discounts

- You've lost all desire to keep up with youthful jargon

- You own a paper address book

- Your children are no longer children

- You feel like it's the morning after even though you haven't been anywhere the night before

YOU STRUGGLE WITH TECHNOLOGY

60s & 70s TRIVIA
(PART 3)

1. Who sang the theme to the 1966 Bond film Thunderball?

2. Which three women played the original 'Charlie's Angels'?

3. Who took 'Billy Don't be a Hero' to number one in the UK in 1974?

4. First broadcast in 1973, it went on to become the longest running TV comedy show in the world, what was its title?

5. What was introduced in 1972 as a means of saving electricity?

6. What's the name of Dolly Parton's 1967 debut album?

7. Which war ended in April 1975 with the fall of Saigon?

8. Which single gave The Eagles their first US number one in 1975?

9. In June 1971 in the US, the 26th Amendment passed giving 18-year-olds what right?

10. Which song gave its name to The Beatles' first full-length film?

(See page 95 for answers)

THE OLDER THE FIDDLER, THE SWEETER THE TUNE.

ENGLISH PROVERB

A WORD FROM THE WISE

The young man knows the rules, but the old man knows the exceptions.
Oliver Wendell Holmes Sr.

Youth can not know how age thinks and feels. But old men are guilty if they forget what it was to be young.
J.K. Rowling

Here is my biggest takeaway after 60 years on the planet: there is great value in being fearless. For too much of my life, I was too afraid, too frightened by it all. That fear is one of my biggest regrets.
Diane Keaton

A man who dares to waste one hour of time has not discovered the value of life.
Charles Darwin

Just remember, when you're over the hill, you begin to pick up speed.
Charles M. Schulz

THINGS TO DO NOW YOU'RE 60

- Drop a bad habit
- Take a gap year
- Write a novel
- Photograph your favourite landscapes
- Travel on the Orient Express
- Take ballroom dancing lessons
- Wear bright colours
- Volunteer at a food bank
- Track down any long lost family members

HOST A
MOVIE NIGHT

YOU'RE HAVING A LAUGH

I need more friends who understand that I still want to be invited but I'm not going.

After forty a woman has to choose between losing her figure or her face. My advice is to keep your face, and stay sitting down.
Barbara Cartland

They are not grey hairs, they are my wisdom highlights!

Pete: Do you like the dictionary I bought you for your 40th birthday?
Steve: Sure. It's a great present but I just can't find the words to thank you enough.

It's never too late to be what you want to be...unless you want to be younger, then you're screwed.

AT 60 YEARS OLD, YOUR BIRTHDAY SUIT REQUIRES REGULAR IRONING.

UNKNOWN

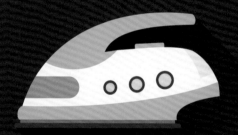

AGE IS NO BARRIER. IT'S A LIMITATION YOU PUT ON YOUR MIND.

JACKIE JOYNER-KERSEE

A WORD FROM THE WISE

Age does not make us childish, as some say; it finds us true children.
Johann Wolfgang von Goethe

By the time you read this, you'll be older than you remember.
Chuck Palahniuk

The idea is to die young…as late as possible.
Unknown

It is a mistake to regard age as a downhill grade toward dissolution. The reverse is true. As one grows older, one climbs with surprising strides.
George Sand

Count your age by the number of memories, not by the number of years.
Unknown

OUR IMMUNE SYSTEMS MAY GET WEAKER AS WE AGE, BUT SCIENCE HAS SHOWN THAT MANY AILMENTS, SUCH AS ALLERGY SYMPTOMS AND MIGRAINES, DECLINE AS WE ENTER LATE MIDDLE AGE.

DID YOU KNOW?

As we get older we tend to be able to manage our emotions more effectively (just as well really; nothing dignified about a grown adult tantruming on a supermarket floor). This was illustrated in a recent study in which participants had to play a gambling game meant to induce regret. Unlike 20-somethings, those in their 60s didn't agonise over losing, and they were less likely to try to redeem their loss by taking big risks later in the game.

The average person tells four lies a day or 1,460 a year, a total of 87,600 by the age of 60. The most common lie? 'I'm fine'.

Contrary to the stereotype of rigid beliefs setting in as we get older, a US study of over 46,000 people over three decades revealed that adults' attitudes got more liberal regarding politics, economics, race, gender, religion and sexuality as they aged.

60 THINGS YOU SHOULD KNOW BY THE TIME YOU TURN 60 (PART 5)

- Your age doesn't define you

- How to love unconditionally

- How to keep evolving

- Be courageous

- Mistakes mould you

- How to look for the good in people

- Be quick to help

- How to laugh at yourself

- How to share

YOU HAVE
TO EXERCISE

AT 61, MOMOFUKU ANDO INVENTED RAMEN CUP NOODLES.

YOU'RE NEVER TOO OLD

It was only after he retired that Frank McCourt decided to write about his childhood, publishing his memoir **Angela's Ashes** at the age of 66.

James Parkinson identified Parkinson's disease when he was 62.

At the age of 69, James Hutton originated the modern theory of the formation of the Earth's crust.

Dame Judi Dench was a distinguished stage actress but she was in her 60s when her movie career began and she became a household name.

YOU KNOW YOU ARE 60 WHEN...

- You write down telephone numbers

- You no longer recognise your own hands - surely they must belong to one of your parents?

- You're no longer afraid of failure

- There's more hair up your nose and in your ears than on your head

- You've let go of a lot of disappointments

- You're considering downsizing

- You've learnt how to say 'no'

- You start your sentences and...err, wait, what was I saying?

YOUR KNEES BUCKLE BUT YOUR BELT WON'T

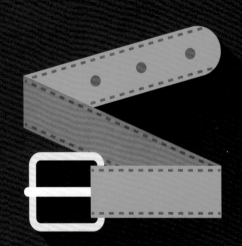

AGE IS WISDOM IF ONE HAS LIVED ONE'S LIFE PROPERLY.

MIRIAM MAKEBA

A WORD FROM THE WISE

Nobody cares how old you are but you. People only care about what you can do, and you can do anything you want, at any age.
Steve Chandler

Is someone different at age 18 or 60? I believe one stays the same.
Hayao Miyazaki

Never use the passing years as an excuse for old age.
Robert Brault

An old young man, will be a young old man.
Benjamin Franklin

The more you praise and celebrate your life, the more there is in life to celebrate.
Oprah Winfrey

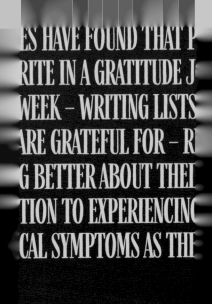

...ES HAVE FOUND THAT P...
...RITE IN A GRATITUDE J...
...WEEK – WRITING LISTS...
...ARE GRATEFUL FOR – R...
...G BETTER ABOUT THE...
...TION TO EXPERIENCIN...
...CAL SYMPTOMS AS TH...

DID YOU KNOW?

Polls suggest that people over the age of 60 report being far less stressed than their younger counterparts, with issues like work, family, money and housing not causing the concern they once did.

As we get older, we tend to be able to deal with social conflicts more effectively. In several age-related studies, subjects in their 60s were far better than younger participants at envisageing differing viewpoints, thinking of multiple resolutions and suggesting compromises.

About a third of people who are 60 or older have some hearing loss. This condition, known as presbycusis, may be due to the loss of sensory receptors in the inner ear.

THINGS TO DO NOW YOU'RE 60

- Embrace new technologies

- Take an exercise class

- Stop doing anything that makes you miserable

- Teach your grandchildren a new skill

- Get political

- Let go of your emotional baggage

- Learn a new craft

- Get a new hairstyle

- Maintain your sense of humour

REDISCOVER READING

HOW CAN THEY SAY MY LIFE ISN'T A SUCCESS? HAVE I NOT FOR MORE THAN SIXTY YEARS GOT ENOUGH TO EAT AND ESCAPED BEING EATEN?

LOGAN PEARSALL SMITH

YOU'RE HAVING A LAUGH

After a man passes sixty, his mischief is mainly in his head.
Washington Irving

Age is getting to know all the ways the world turns, so that if you cannot turn the world the way you want, you can at least get out of the way so you won't get run over.
Miriam Makeba

Birthdays are good for you. The more you have, the longer you live!

Congratulations, you've finally reached the wonder years... wonder where your car is parked? Wonder where you left your phone? Wonder where your glasses are? Wonder what day it is?

I've reached an age where my train of thought often leaves the station without me.

WE AGE NOT BY YEARS BUT BY STORIES.

MAZA-DOHTA

A WORD FROM THE WISE

The older we grow the greater becomes our wonder at how much ignorance one can contain without bursting one's clothes.
Mark Twain

If only youth had the knowledge and old age the strength.
Proverb

The young are beautiful - but the old are more beautiful than the young.
Walt Whitman

The older one grows, the more one likes indecency.
Virginia Woolf

When people talk about the good old days, I say to people, 'It's not the days that are old, it's you that's old.' I hate the good old days. What is important is that today is good.
Karl Lagerfeld

YOU'RE NEVER TOO OLD

At 68, Lillian Carter, President Carter's mother, joined the Peace Corps and spent the next two years working as a nurse in India.

At 69, Canadian Ed Whitlock of Milton, Ontario, became the oldest person to run a standard marathon in under three hours.

At 62, J.R.R. Tolkien published the first volume in his fantasy series, **The Lord of the Rings.**

A. C. Bhaktivedanta Swami Prabhupada, founder of the Hare Krishna movement, was 69 years old before he started the International Society for Krishna Consciousness.

SIR ALEXANDER FLEMING WAS 64 YEARS OLD WHEN HE WAS AWARDED THE NOBEL PRIZE FOR HIS DISCOVERY OF PENICILLIN.

60 THINGS YOU SHOULD KNOW BY THE TIME YOU TURN 60 (PART 6)

- How to laugh every day
- When to walk away from negative relationships
- How to express gratitude
- How to pamper yourself
- That you are strong enough to make it through the tough times
- To look people in the eye
- You don't have to win every argument
- Silence is golden
- There's no such thing as a free lunch

ROMANCE STILL EXISTS

THINGS TO DO
NOW YOU'RE 60

- Start your own business
- Get in shape
- Edit your friendship groups
- Paint a self-portrait
- Re-invigorate your wardrobe
- Host a street party
- Keep up-to-date with current affairs
- Visit faraway friends
- Consider a tattoo

CRUISE ALONG ROUTE 66

60s & 70s TRIVIA
(PART 4)

1. Electric Light Orchestra formed in 1970 in which city?

2. 1974 saw the first sale of what kitchen appliance to UK homes?

3. Who headlined the 1969 Isle of Wight festival, his first major appearance since a motorcycle accident in 1966?

4. Which 1968 movie co-starred a computer named H.A.L.?

5. Which singer-songwriter, considered by many to be the greatest electric guitar player of all time, died in 1970?

6. Which British university opened its doors for the first time in January 1971, welcoming 25,000 students?

7. Which Monkees track provided Robert Wyatt with a hit in 1974?

8. Which bluesy rock singer was discovered at the Monterey Pop Festival in 1967?

9. What happened during the Men's singles final at Wimbledon in 1973 for the first time?

10. Who were 'Guilty' in the UK top ten in 1974?

(See page 96 for answers)

YOU'RE NEVER TOO OLD

Winston Churchill became Prime Minister at the age of 64.

At 62, John Wayne won an Oscar for his role in True Grit.

General Dwight Eisenhower was 62 when he became president, and passed his 70th birthday in office.

Physicist Sir William Crookes invented the first instruments to study radioactivity when he was 68.

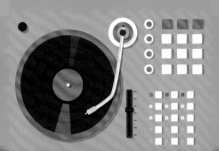

N RUTH FLOWERS HI
DECIDED TO FOLLOW
EAMS AND BECOME A
ENJOYED SUCCESS L
IFE AS DJ 'MAMY RO

A MAJOR ADVANTAGE OF AGE IS LEARNING TO ACCEPT PEOPLE WITHOUT PASSING JUDGMENT.

LIZ CARPENTER

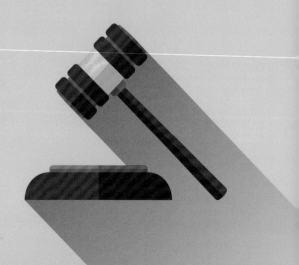

A WORD FROM THE WISE

... forty's nothing, at fifty you're in your prime, sixty's the new forty, and so on.
Julian Barnes

The older I get, the more I meet people, the more convinced I am that we must only work on ourselves, to grow in grace. The only thing we can do about other people is to love them.
Dorothy Day

The person who has lived the most is not the one with the most years but the one with the richest experiences.
Jean-Jacques Rousseau

The best age is the age you are.
Maggie Kuhn

Those who love deeply never grow old; they may die of old age, but they die young.
Benjamin Franklin

ANSWERS: 60s & 70s TRIVIA

(PART 1)

1. The Ed Sullivan Show
2. Twiggy
3. Rupert Murdoch
4. 1968
5. Che Guevara
6. Matt Monro
7. Madison Square Gardens
8. Carrie
9. Richard Nixon
10. Woodstock

(PART 2)

1. The Kray brothers
2. 1965
3. Caernarfon Castle
4. Butch Cassidy and the Sundance Kid
5. Jacqueline Kennedy Onassis
6. Abbey Road
7. Apollo 13
8. Wrigley's Chewing Gum
9. Albatross
10. Patty Hearst

(PART 3)

1. Tom Jones
2. Kate Jackson, Farrah Fawcett and Jaclyn Smith
3. Paper Lace
4. Last of the Summer Wine

5. Three day week

6. Hello, I'm Dolly

7. Vietnam

8. 'Best of My Love'

9. The right to vote

10. 'A Hard Day's Night'

(PART 4)

1. Birmingham

2. Microwave

3. Bob Dylan

4. 2001: A Space Odyssey

5. Jimi Hendrix

6. The Open University

7. 'I'm a Believer'

8. Janis Joplin

9. A tie-break had to be played

10. The Pearls